level 3

TECHNIC
LESSONS

by JAMES BASTIEN

Ed. WP14
$2.25

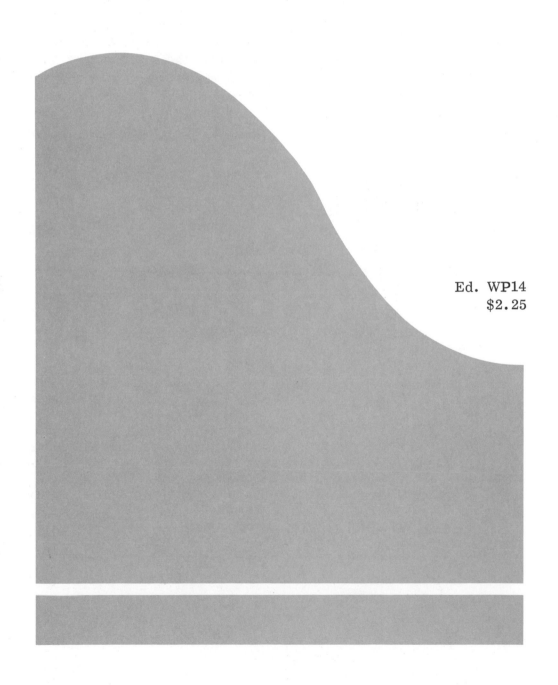

THE BASTIEN PIANO LIBRARY

KJOS WEST · Neil A. Kjos. Jr. Publisher · San Diego. California

TO THE TEACHER

TECHNIC LESSONS, Level 3, is designed to be used simultaneously with **PIANO LESSONS, Level 3** (© *1976 KJOS WEST, San Diego, California. Ed. No. WP4*). It may also be used with any piano course.

DYNAMICS Unless indicated, the dynamics are to be suggested by the teacher. On each repeat of the exercise, have the student use a different dynamic level.

TEMPO Direct the student to play each exercise in three tempos: slow, medium and fast. On each repeat, have the student use a different tempo.

TOUCH Some exercises have specific directions to practice both legato and staccato. Many of the legato exercises (those with slurs) may also be played staccato at the teacher's discretion.

TRANSPOSITION Transposition is indicated for some exercises. Additional transposition for these exercises may be suggested at the teacher's discretion.

The goal of **TECHNIC LESSONS** is to develop hand finger coordination and facility, and to develop ease and control at the keyboard. A variety of keys and keyboard experiences is provided to give the student a basic foundation in elementary fundamentals.

Suggested Use of Materials with "PIANO LESSONS, Level 3."

When the student reaches **page 5,** he is ready to begin__Theory Lessons - Level 3 (WP9)
When the student reaches **page 9,** he is ready to begin__Technic Lessons - Level 3 (WP14)
When the student reaches **page 11,** he is ready to begin_____Piano Solos - Level 3 (WP25)
When the student reaches **page 15,** he is ready to begin__Sight Reading - Level 3 (WP18)
When the student reaches **page 17,** he is ready to begin____First Hanon Studies - Level 3 (WP31)

SHEET MUSIC from **Level Three Solos** may be assigned to the student at the teacher's discretion.

TO THE STUDENT

The studies in this book are designed to help you play the piano with ease and control. Allow time each day for technic practice. You might use these studies as warm-ups before beginning to practice your pieces.

Think of these three points often.

HEIGHT

Sit up high enough to reach the keys easily. Your wrists and forearms should be in a *straight line* over the keys.

POSTURE

Sit up *straight* in front of the center of the piano. Place your feet flat on the floor.

HAND POSITION

When playing the piano, hold your fingers in a nice *curved shape*.

CONTENTS

MAJOR~MINOR FIVE FINGER POSITIONS

THE RACE

1st time—*legato*
2nd time—*staccato*

I   tonic
IV   sub-dominant
V   dominant

G major scale – F#
2 octaves

MINOR FIVE FINGER POSITIONS

MOUNTAIN CLIMBING

legato—staccato

BROKEN CHORD BASS~1ST STYLE

Feb. 8

WARM~UP

Transpose to other keys.

LITTLE WALTZ

SMOOTH SAILING

BROKEN CHORD BASS ~ 2ND STYLE

WARM-UP

Transpose to other keys.

SCALING IN C

SCALING IN G

PHRASING STUDIES

SHIFTING GEARS

WALTZ FOR JOHANN

TRIADS OF THE SCALE

WARM-UP

TAP-DANCE

CASTANETS

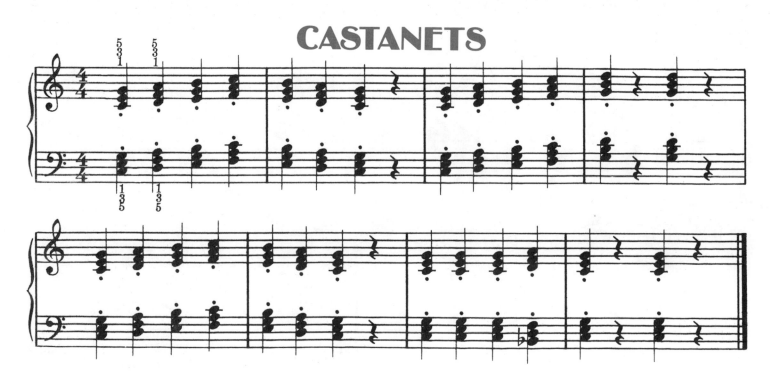

FREIGHT TRAIN

GOING UP HILL

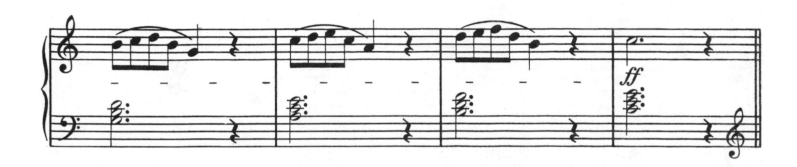

COMING DOWN HILL

LEGER LINE AND SPACE NOTE ETUDES

IN AN OLD CASTLE

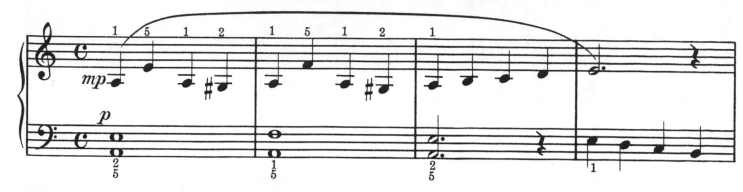

JOGGING

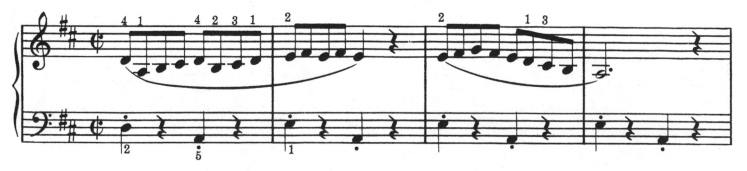

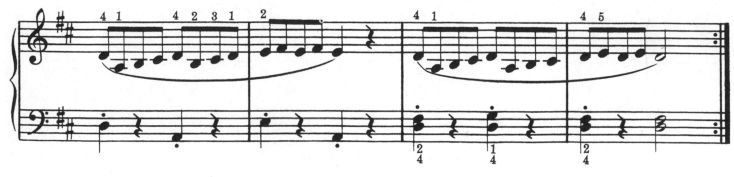

HOP O' MY THUMB

TEETER-TOTTER

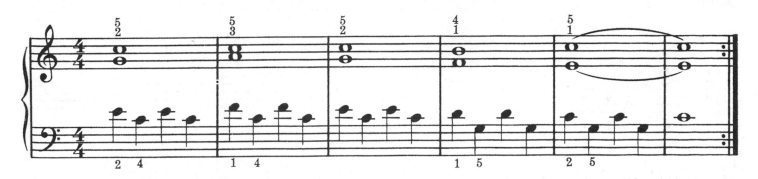

SING A SONG

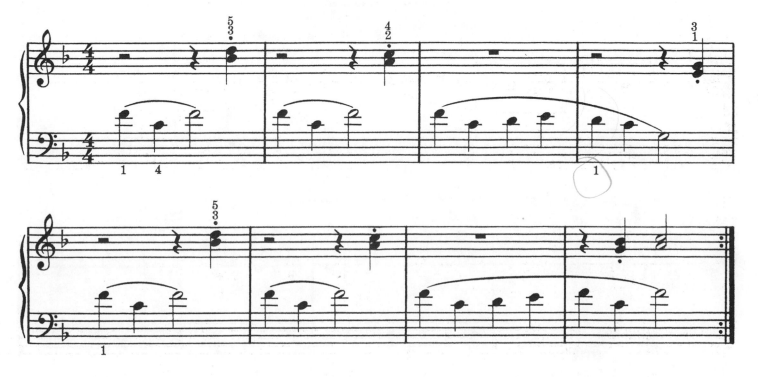

14

LEGATO~STACCATO TOUCHES COMBINED

ON THE TRAPEZE

THE HUMMINGBIRD

PHRASING STUDIES

HIPPOS AT PLAY

ELEPHANTS' PARADE

TRIPLET RHYTHM STUDIES

RIPPLES ON THE WATER

Transpose to other keys.

4TH OF JULY ROCKETS

HIT THE MARK!

OVER THE HURDLES

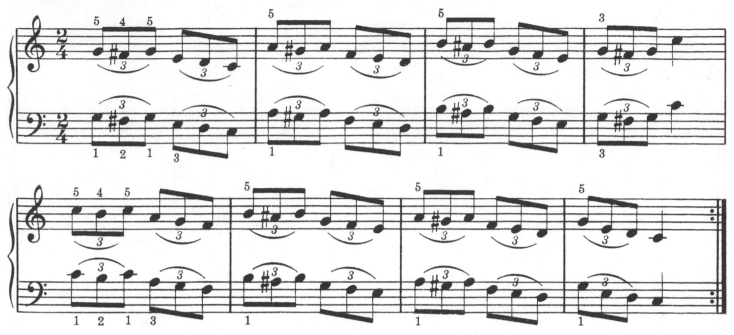

SPEEDY GONZALES

WP 14

MINOR SCALE STUDIES

1.

A minor—Contrary Motion

2.

A minor—Primary Chords

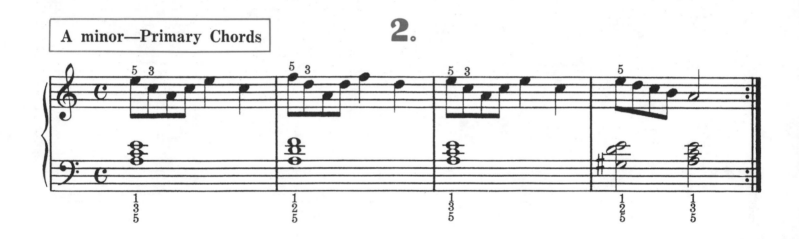

ETUDE IN A MINOR

1.

D minor—Contrary Motion

2.

D minor—Primary Chords

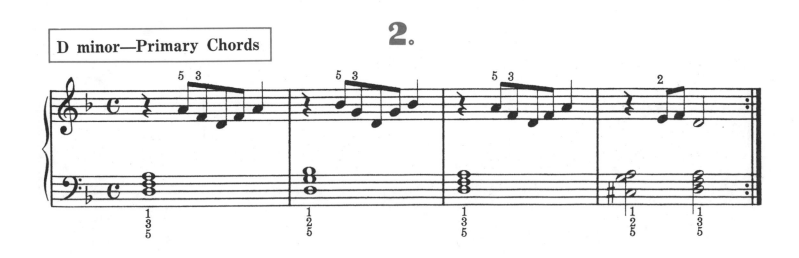

ETUDE IN D MINOR

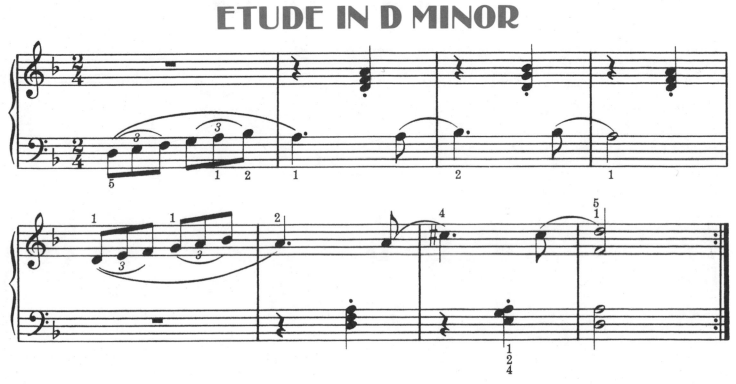

E minor—Contrary Motion

1.

E minor—Primary Chords

2.

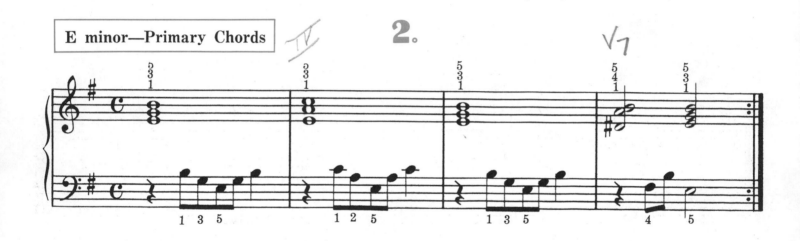

ETUDE IN E MINOR

CHROMATIC SCALE STUDIES

CRAB CRAWLING

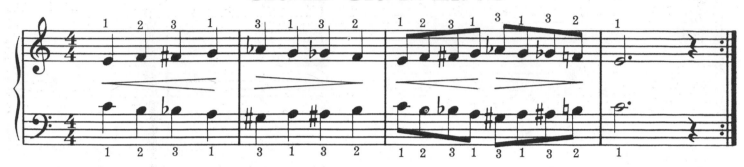

THE WIND

HAUNTED HOUSE

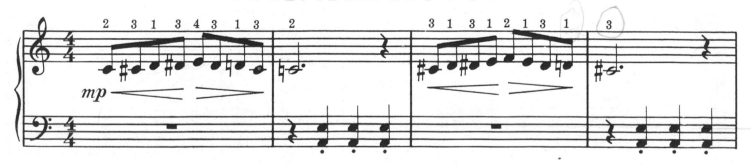

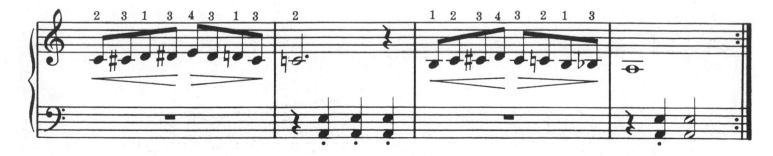

TRIAD AND INVERSION STUDIES

1.

Transpose to other Major keys.

2.

Transpose to other minor keys.

3.

Transpose to other Major and minor keys.

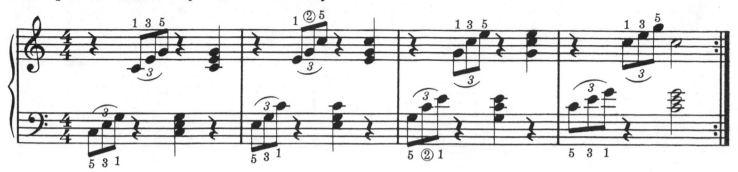

Transpose to other Major and minor keys.

4.

BUGLES IN THE NIGHT

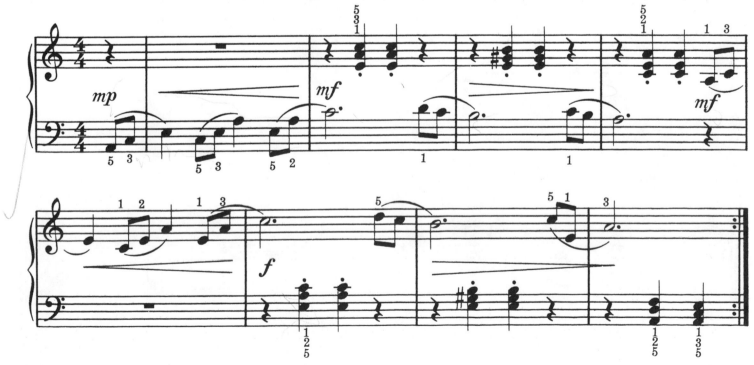

WP14

ETUDE IN G

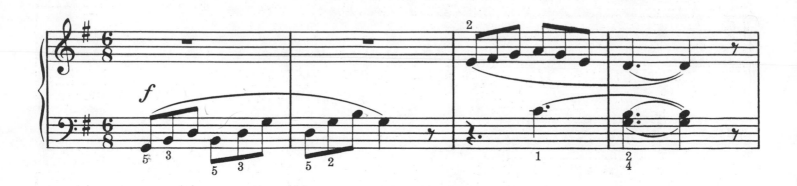

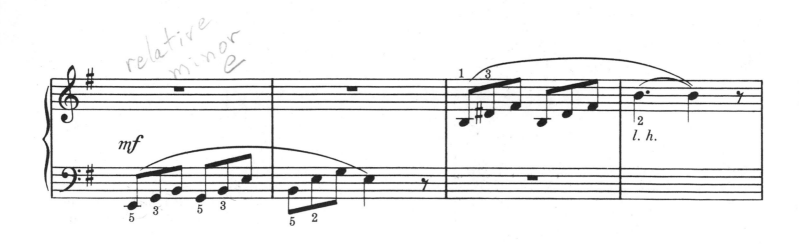

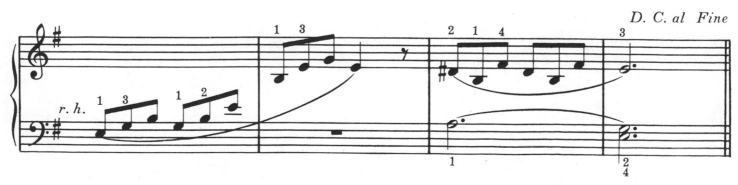

BUSY FINGERS

Transpose to other keys.

DOUBLE NOTE STUDIES

1.

Continue this pattern
up the keyboard
on the white keys.

2.

legato

Continue this pattern
up the keyboard
on the white keys.

WP 14

D♭ MAJOR SCALE STUDIES

1.

2.

PRIMARY CHORDS IN D♭ MAJOR

WARM-UPS

AT THE BEACH

A SUNNY DAY

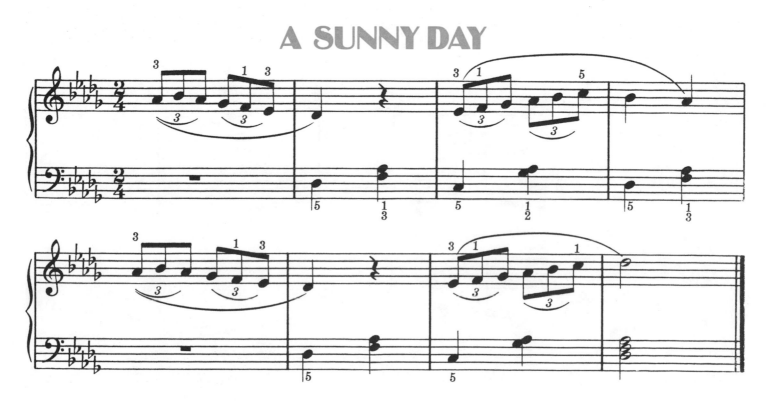

A♭ MAJOR SCALE STUDIES

1.

legato—staccato

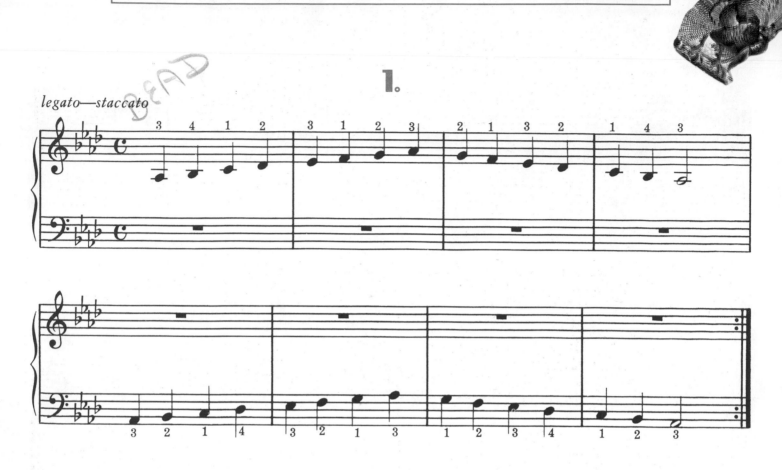

2.

PRIMARY CHORDS IN A♭ MAJOR

WARM~UPS

BIKE RIDE

ONE O'CLOCK JUMP

E♭ MAJOR SCALE STUDIES

1.

legato—staccato

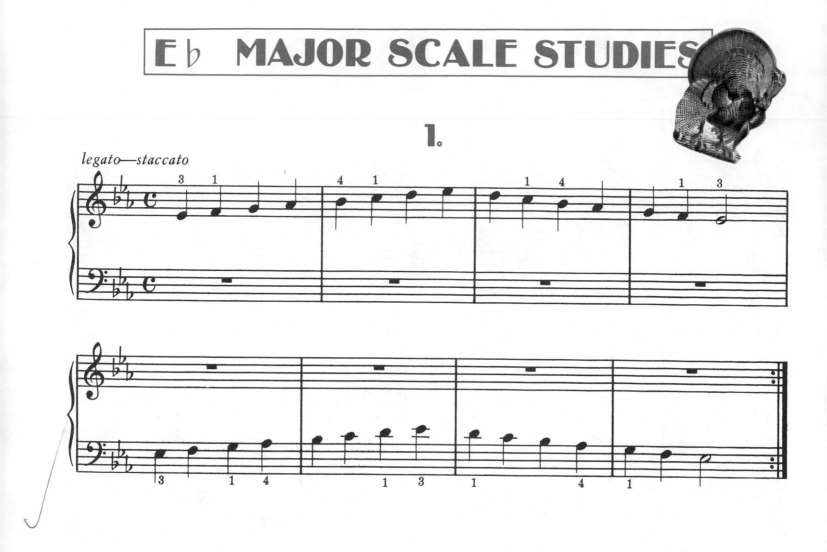

2.

PRIMARY CHORDS IN E♭ MAJOR

cadence

WARM~UPS

THE BANJO

QUICK ROCK

FINGER EXTENSION STUDIES

1.

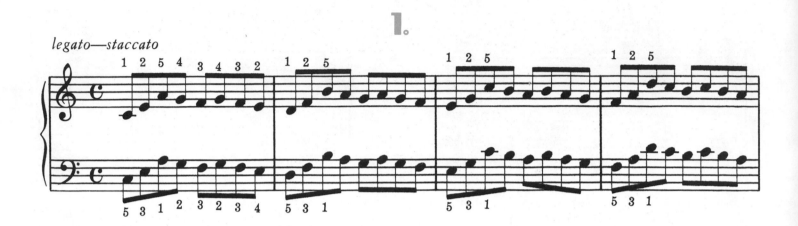

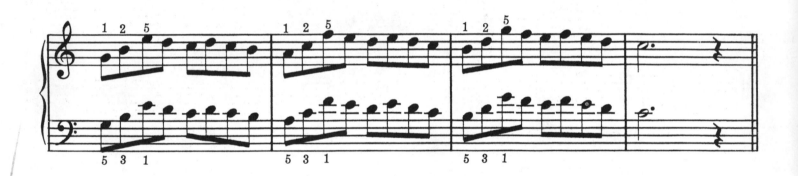

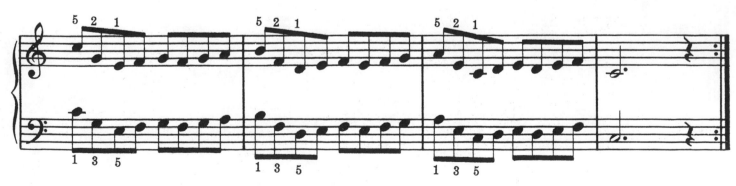

2.

legato—staccato

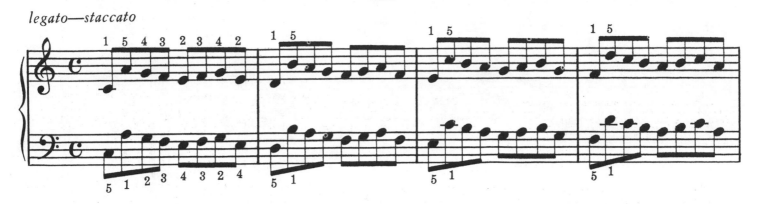

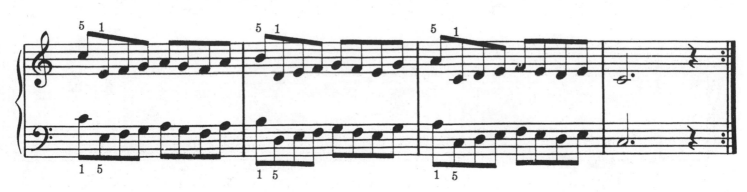

TWO OCTAVE MAJOR SCALES
SHARP SCALES

TWO OCTAVE MAJOR SCALES
FLAT SCALES

TEACHER'S TECHNIC

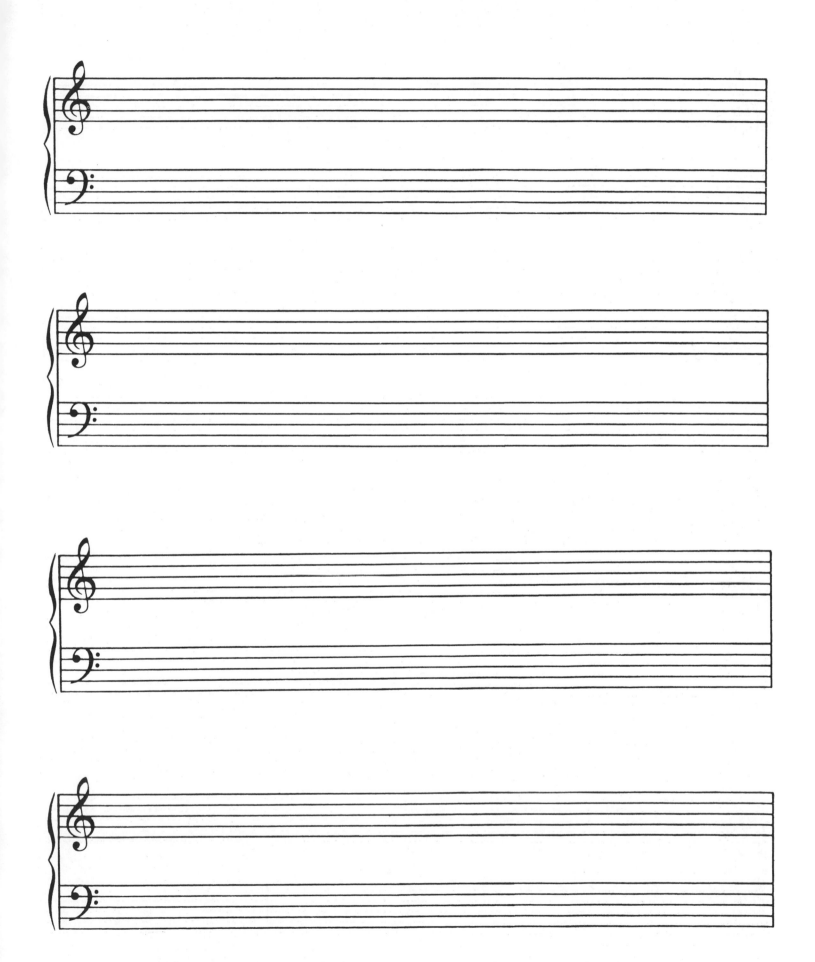

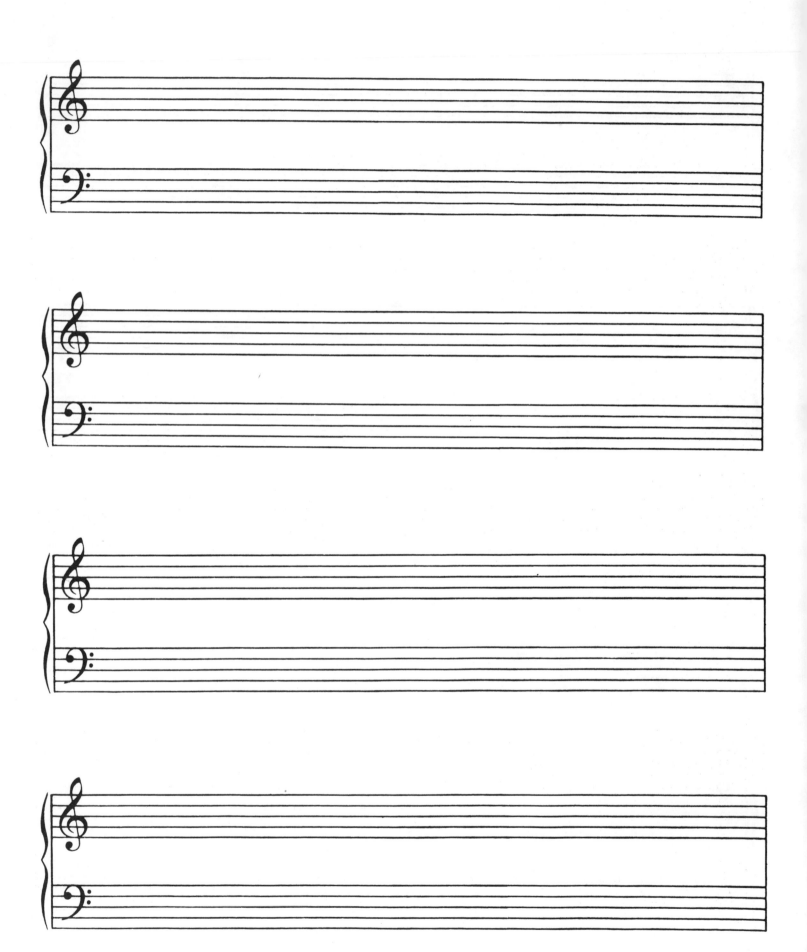

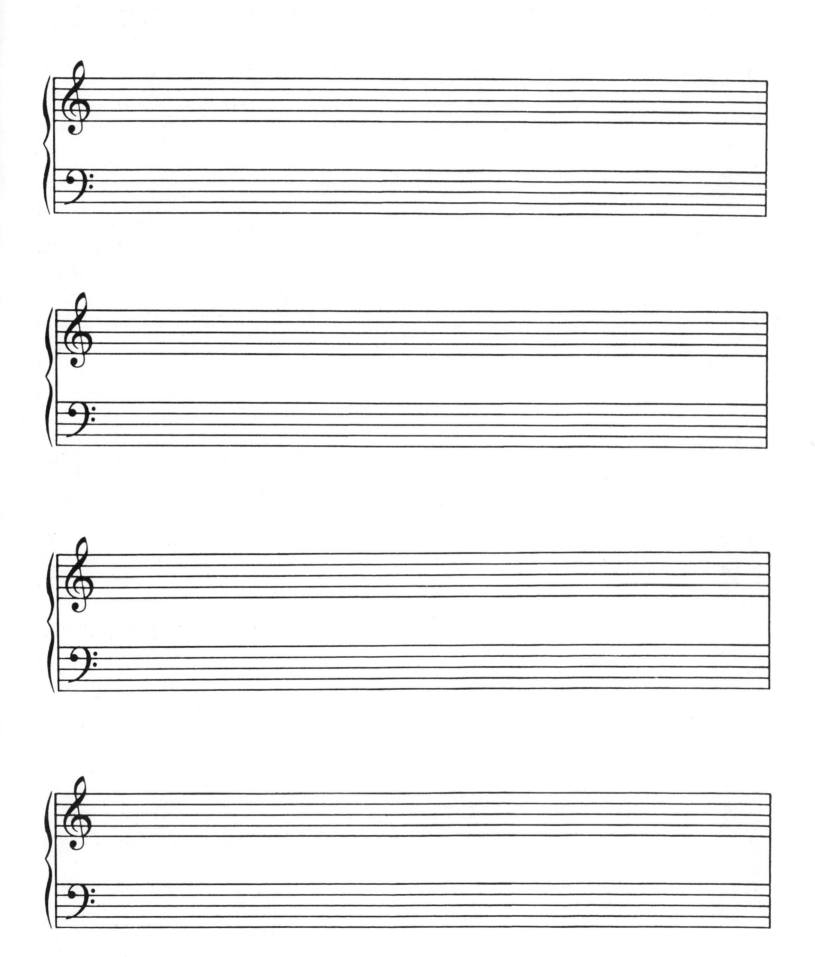